I0843588

Table of Contents

INTRODUCTION

INTRODUCTION

From the time we are born, many will be educated to be a version of themselves that please others. Whether it comes from the way you were raised or how you were taught in school, we often learn to put a mask on and be an actor in our life.

Unfortunately, that behavior will not lead you to be happy and live a fulfilling life. You can discover the best version of yourself and transform your life so that you are no longer an actor in your life. Choose to live the life that was made for you.

To get the most out of this book, you will have to explore yourself, be aware of your actions and thoughts of your behaviors, and be honest with yourself. This book is for you, and no one other than yourself can know who you are.

With commitment, vulnerability, and curiosity, you will be able to become best version of yourself and put away the mask that you've worn for much too long. Are you ready to claim your power?

Then let's start to explore your current life and see how much you are currently true to yourself!

"The power you have is to be the best version of yourself you can be so that you can create a better world."
Ashley Rickards

CHAPTER 1
BEING YOURSELF

CHAPTER 1: BEING YOURSELF

The best version of yourself is being true to yourself, but what does this mean? It is sometimes easier to explain something by identifying what it isn't. That said, here's a list of what is not being the best version of yourself:

Being true to yourself is not about pleasing others;

Being true to yourself is not about hurting others;

Being true to yourself is not about doing things you dislike;

Being true to yourself is not about forcing yourself to do something;

Being true to yourself is not about being hard on yourself;

Being true to yourself is not about judging others and comparing yourself;

Being true to yourself is not about being a victim of your surroundings;

Being true to yourself is not about acting in away that will attract more fans on social media.

Being true to yourself means that you behave and communicate with complete integrity in your belief, values, and, most of all, with what feels right in your heart. When there is an alignment with your inner self (emotions, states, and desires) and outer self (behaviors, communication, and relationships), you are being the best version of yourself.

Assessing Yourself

Have you ever felt like your behavior and the way that you held yourself varied depending on who is around you and where you are?

We tend to play a different role when we are with individuals that we want to please or want to make sure that they like us. For example, you might behave in a completely different way if you are at work or with people you just met and want to be friends with them. We tend to be ourselves when we are at home or with childhood friends. That is when we let our guards down and become more vulnerable and less worried about how others might perceive us.

The following questions will help you identify which area of your life you are

the best version of yourself. Answer yes or no, pick the answer the closest to how you feel (mostly yes or mostly no).

Business, Career and Professional World		
	YES	NO
Are you satisfied with your work?		
Do you get along with your colleagues?		
Do you know what you want to do for work?		
Are you comfortable with your knowledge and skills?		
Do you feel you are contributing to the world in a way that fulfills you?		
Are you happy in your career?		
Given the opportunity to change work, would you still stay in your job?		
TOTAL:		
Love and Romantic Relationship		
	YES	NO
Are you experiencing happiness in love?		
Do you feel like you can be yourself in a love relationship?		
Do you feel loved for who you truly are?		

	YES	NO
Do you feel your partner knows you very well?		
Are your needs mostly met in your love relationship?		
Is it easy for you to understand your partner?		
Are you healthily independent in your love relationship?		
TOTAL:		

Family

	YES	NO
Are you close to your family?		
Do you feel like you have a connection with your family?		
Can you be yourself around your family?		
Do you mostly experience positive emotions around your family?		
Is being with your family where you feel like you are truly yourself?		
Do you feel supported by your family?		
Can you count on your family when you need help?		
TOTAL:		

Friends

	YES	NO
Do you have a close bond with your friends?		
Do you trust your friends?		
Would you say that the level of "give and take" in your friendship is balanced between you and them?		
Do you feel like you can be yourself with all your friends?		
Do you have healthy boundaries with your friends?		
Do you feel comfortable saying "no" to your friends?		
Are you honest with your friends?		
TOTAL:		

Acquaintances and Neighbors

	YES	NO
Are you honest with people you meet for the first time?		
Do you stay true to yourself when you meet new people? (Meaning you don't change your demeanor.)		
Are you honest with yourself when you meet someone new that you don't like? (Meaning you don't try to convince yourself that you need to give them a chance.)		

	YES	NO
Are you the type of person that will say "no" to an offer to go out if you don't feel like hanging out with that person?		
When you meet someone, do you immediately know if you will get along with them or not?		
Are you able to distance yourself from a person when you are not interested in their friendship?		
Are you comfortable expressing your thoughts with unfamiliar people?		
TOTAL:		
Self		
	YES	NO
Are you comfortable in your own skin?		
Do you appreciate your physical body?		
Would you say you have healthy self-talk?		
Are you comfortable with compliments from others?		
Is it easy for you to accept help from others?		
Do you appreciate spending time by yourself?		
Could you list ten qualities about yourself right now?		
TOTAL:		
Compile all the "yes" and "no" from each section. TOTAL:		

The more "yes" you have, the easier it is for you to be yourself. The goal is to be your true self in all spheres of your life. Based on that quick survey, which area of your life has more "NO" answers? Keep that in mind; I hope that by the end of reading this book, you are more comfortable being yourself in that area of your life.

"Every decision you make reflects your evaluation of who you are."
Marianne Williamson

CHAPTER 2
PROJECTING YOURSELF

CHAPTER 2: PROJECTING YOURSELF

Some of the questions in the previous chapter might not make sense to you. For example, we asked if you are "the type of person that will say 'no' to an offer to go out if you don't feel like hanging out with that person." If it is hard for you to say "no" to others and instead of saying "no," you use "white lies," which means that you are also able to tell yourself "white lies." Being dishonest is one of the most common mistakes we make in life that keeps the best version of ourselves at bay.

It takes a long time to realize that the external world is a projection of what is happening internally. Since the external world is a pure reflection of us, it can give us a lot of information about ourselves when we take the time to observe and be aware.

For example, if you hate your job, it could be a sign that you technically don't recognize your skills and abilities. That you are unable to clearly see what you are capable of and therefore settle for jobs that you dislike. It's almost like you are creating your own misery.

Take a moment to list some of the things that you dislike in your environment. That could be the way that your romantic partner treats you, the way that your family makes you feel about yourself or your professional life.

If I could change something about my life, it would be the following:

____

____

____

____

____

____

Now that you've listed a few things you would like to change about your life. Let's reflect on what this means regarding yourself.

Here are a few examples of what could potentially be the projection.

External Projection	Internal Reality
My romantic partner doesn't give me enough attention.	I am struggling to provide myself with love and care.
My friends don't listen to me or don't want to hear from me; it's always about them.	I tend to forget about my needs and always try to please others. I have a hard time putting myself as a priority.
I'm still stuck doing stuff that I don't like. It seems to always be like that. Why can't others do the things I like?	I am unable to say "no" and have not created healthy boundaries with others. I am not able to respect mys elf .
I've always hated my jobs and can't seem to find what I want to do in my career.	I am unable to see my skills and abilities. I tend to be hard on myself. I'm never good enough.

External Projection	Internal Reality
When I'm on social media, I want people to like my post. I can take 100s of pictures before I get to the perfect one to share on my social media.	I perceive myself as not enough, and I feel I need to be perfect to be loved. I don't accept myself for who I am. I need the approval of others to like myself.
Every romantic partner I had, I did everything they wanted and always tried to please them, but they never gave the same amount of effort in the relationship. Why is it that I can't get what I offer?	I believe that I cannot be loved for myself. Therefore, I have to be another person to be liked. I have to act in a certain way to receive love.

Now, your turn to dig deep and find what your external world is telling you about your internal reality:

External Projection	Internal Reality

External Projection	Internal Reality

What have you learned about yourself in that activity? Are there aspects of you that you want to work on? Are there some projections that you would like to address and change the cycle in your life?

In the next chapter, we will look at things that make you reactive. Reactivity is often another aspect that needs our awareness. When we learn our triggers, we learn about our true selves and what needs to heal within to be the best version of ourselves.

"You don't see the world as it is, you see it according to who you are."
Stephen Covey

CHAPTER 3
LEARNING YOUR TRIGGERS

CHAPTER 3: LEARNING YOUR TRIGGERS

Do you avoid certain subjects with others because you know you'll be angry or frustrated? Are you sometimes easily offended by others? When you become aware of your triggers, you will be able to move from being reactive to being at peace with what others think when it differs from your opinion.

When we are triggered by something external to us, we tend to blame others for what we are experiencing. Blaming others for what we are experiencing is living a victim mindset. Getting out of that mindset will be easier once you stop reacting to others and the faster your mindset will shift to be more in alignment with your true self.

First, you have to accept that the only things you can change in this world are your behavior, your mindset, and the way you communicate or interact with others. As you probably know by now, you have no control over other people's behavior or mind. Make decisions now that you will no longer blame your problems on external factors.

Second, learn to be aware of your behavior and thoughts, especially when you go in that space of blaming others or reacting to what they do or say.

Start by making a list of what you feel trigger you.
Some examples could be politics, injustice, self-centered people, incompetence, etc. Try to be as specific as possible by using an example to explain the trigger.

I tend to react emotionally to the following:

____

____

____

____

____

____

____

____

Now make a plan to react differently in the future when those situations or subjects arise. How will you better handle your emotions in these situations?

Another approach to this would be to try to understand why you get so reactive to those situations or subjects. Here are a few examples and what it could mean for a person.

Trigger	Internal Reality
I get so offended when people accuse me of being selfish or self-centered.	I tend to feel like others have it better than me. Therefore, I feel like I don't get what I deserve, and when I focus on my needs, it's because I want what others have.
I get so annoyed when someone talks about women's rights; I just can't stand it.	I feel like it's always been about a woman in my life. When are we going to realize that I am important too, and I deserve what others also deserve?
My partner tells me that I don't give him enough attention and that he feels lonely when we are together.	That makes me so angry because I need my time alone too and he doesn't give me any space, we are always together. I try to ignore him and have my space, but that doesn't work either.
I can't talk about politics; the current situation makes me so mad.	The current political situation is bringing up some deep wounds from past experiences I haven't dealt with in my life.

Now your turn, what triggers you, and when you explore this more profoundly, what does it say about your internal reality?

Trigger	Internal Reality

In order to become the best version of yourself, you must tame the shadows that have been stalking you for a long time. It's not always easy, but when you face your dark side, you bring it to light and immediately allow yourself to shine brighter than ever! It gives you the space to heal deep wounds.

Taking responsibility for your own happiness starts by recognizing your responsibility in your life and stop giving your powers to others. When you blame others, you do not own your responsibility in your life. For example, if you continuously blame external factors for the life that you live, you are giving up your powers and will to others. You are allowing others to dictate your behavior and mindset.

In doing so, you separate yourself completely from yourself and become a robot just going through the motions in life. If you want to be yourself, you have to take ownership of your life. Start by being aware when you blame others for the situation you are in and shift your mindset to solution finding and own the solution that will get you out of a difficult situation. It's time for you to take back your powers and choose to live the life that you want! When you can maintain a healthy mindset and break the bad habit of reacting to anything, you become more at peace within and better apt to be your best self.

In the next chapter, we will explore your limiting beliefs and how you can transform them to be more empowering. Those limiting beliefs are often connected to deep wounds from the past that we carry with us for years.

"The feeling of being offended is a warning indicator that is showing you where to look within yourself for unresolved issues."
Bryant McGill

CHAPTER 4
KNOCKING DOWN YOUR BARRIERS

CHAPTER 4: KNOCKING DOWN YOUR BARRIERS

There are plenty of reasons why a person would not want to be themselves fully. According to the Physician and Psychiatrist Dr. John Pierrakos, there are main experiences that create barriers to be our true selves. These barriers are five wounds, were popularized by the famous French author, Lise Bourbeau. Those wounds are abandonment, rejection, injustice, humiliation, and betrayal.

Let's start with a quick assessment that will help you determine which wounds are the most significant barriers to your growth and expression of your true self.

	YES	NO
Do you feel like a victim regularly? (A)		
As a child, did you ever feel that you were not wanted? (R)		
Do you lack self-confidence? (A, R, H, I)		
Do you regularly seek solitude? (R)		
Do you do the tasks slowly? (H)		
Do you find it difficult to ask for help? (I)		
Do you think you're stable and very responsible? (B)		
Do you want to be important in life? (B)		
Do you regularly doubt your choices? (I)		
Do you stress or get nervous before you speak? (R, I)		
Do you feel anxious before you go on a trip, facing a change in your life? (A)		
Do you use drugs or alcohol all the time? (R, A, H)		

Do you like acting? (B)		
Do you always need a presence around you? (A)		
Do you feel the need to help others all the time? (A, H, B)		
Are you regularly convinced you are right? Do you try to convince others? (B)		
Are you demanding on yourself? (B, I)		
Do you like everything to be in order around you? (B, I)		
Do you generally distrust others? (R, B, I)		
Do you take care of other people's problems before you take care of your own? Do you take care of others more easily than yourself? (H)		
Do you often blame yourself; do you regularly feel guilty? (R, A, H, I)		
Do you regularly have breathing problems? (R, A, H)		
Do you often have low blood sugar? Do you have diabetes? (R, A, H)		
Do you often have body tensions? (B, I)		
Are you hypersensitive to being dirty (take a few showers a day, hate having hands dirty, etc.)? (H)		
Do you easily give up a project, a goal along the way? (R, A)		
Are you impatient, refusing the slowness of others? (B, I)		
Are you bulimic? Or do you struggle with an eating disorder? (H)		

SCORING				
CALCULATE ALL THE YES FOR EACH LETTER				
(R) REJECTION	(I) INJUSTICE	(H) HUMILIATION	(A) ABANDONMENT	(B) BETRAYAL
/10	/10	/10	/10	/10

Now that you can see which wound has the most yes out of 10. Let's explore each one of those obstacles in your life and help you understand those deep wounds. Even if you didn't score high on some wounds, read the content because you might still relate with some of the information provided below.

Rejection

The one who suffer rejection feels rejected as a person as well as in his right to exist. Therefore, it is practically impossible to be yourself when you wear that wound. It is not unusual for people who feel rejected to have a fleeing physique, that is to say, a body or a part of the body that seems to want to disappear or become very small. As if the receding person wanted to go unnoticed for fear of being rejected.

In terms of behavior, they often doubt their right to exist. They seek solitude because if they receive a lot of attention, they would be afraid of not knowing what to do. They can be fleeing, which is why they prefer not to get attached to material things because they would prevent them from running away. They often wonder what they are doing on this planet and finds it hard to believe that they could be happy here and bring something to this world.

They don't know what to do with themselves when they get too much attention. In relationships with others, they are constantly finding ways to seek love from the parent of the same sex and will reject themselves from a person of the other sex, often feeling guilty when they face rejection. It is not unusual for them to live in ambivalence; when they are accepted, they won't believe it and often create a self-sabotaging situation so that others reject them. Their biggest fear is panic and anxiety because that often arises in them when they are rejected.

won't believe it and often create a self-sabotaging situation so that others reject them. Their biggest fear is panic and anxiety because that often arises in them when they are rejected.

Injustice

The wound related to injustice is intimately linked to the wound of rejection. While rejection touches deeply the "being," the wound of injustice touches on having and doing. People who have that wound often keeps their body rigid, and as perfect as possible. They have a well-proportioned body; Rigid movements; Stiff neck; and very proud.

They are usually lively with dynamic movements, but also someone who is rigid and lacks flexibility. Often a perfectionist and envious. These persons tend to cut themselves off from their feelings and often cross their arms. They try to be seem perfect and justify themselves a lot. They find it difficult to admit that they have problems. They often doubt their choices. They like order and tend to control themselves by demanding a lot from others. They can be angry and cold and has difficulty showing affection. They don't want to be late but will often be delayed because they take a long time to prepare.

It is often difficult for people with the injustice wound to accept compliments, help, or gifts from others because they feel in debt toward the person after. Their biggest fear is when others are cold toward them because that awakens the unfairness but is also a reflection of themselves.

Humiliation

This wound is mostly related to the physical aspect of having and doing. Most individuals with the humiliation wound have a larger round body, round face, with a broad and rounded neck.

They are often ashamed of themselves and others or afraid to shame others. They think they are dirty or unclean. They don't want to recognize and assume their sensuality and their love of the pleasures associated with the senses. That is why they often compensate and reward themselves with food. And they gain weight quickly to give themselves a reason not to enjoy their senses. They are also afraid of being "punished" if they enjoy life too much. So, they ignore their freedom by putting the needs of others before their own, so that they stop enjoying life.

Most individuals with the humiliation wound want to do everything for others. In reality, they want to create constraints and obligations for themselves to stop enjoying their freedom and life. This lack of enjoyment reinforces the feeling of being abused and humiliated. And in the same way, they tend to demean and humiliate others by making them feel that they cannot do it alone without them. They are often inclined to blame themselves for everything and even take the blame for others. Their biggest fear is their freedom; they are afraid to lose the ability to be themselves when humiliated by others.

Abandonment

The wound experienced in the case of abandonment is the second deepest after that of rejection because they both affect the being at a profound level.

Most people with the abandonment wound lack vigor. Their body is usually long and slender with a back that becomes rounded and sagging. As if the spine and muscles were not able to keep the body upright. Their body seems to need help to hold on.

Those who suffer from abandonment do not feel emotionally nourished enough. They need constant help and support. They think that they cannot do anything on their own and regularly needs someone to support them. They often have ups and downs: for a while, they are happy, and everything is fine, and suddenly, they feel unhappy and sad. They tend to dramatize a lot: the smallest little incident takes on gigantic proportions. In a group, they like to talk about themselves and often brings everything back to them.

Besides, they usually seek the opinion or approval of others before making decisions. They can't make up their mind, or they doubt their choice when they don't feel supported by someone else. And when they do something for someone, they do it with the expectation of a return of affection. Their problems give them the gift of attention, and this prevents them from being abandoned. The more a person acts like a victim, the more his or her abandonment wound increases. Their greatest fear is loneliness since it is directly connected to that feeling of being abandoned.

Betrayal (or Treason)

The wound of betrayal is intimately related to the wound of abandonment).
While abandonment is about being, the wound of betrayal is about having
and doing.

Their body often exhibits strength and power. In men: shoulders wider than
the lower body. In women: lower body larger than the shoulders (pear-
shaped body). The higher the asymmetry between the upper and lower
body, the greater the betrayal wound.

Very uncompromising, they want to show others what they are capable of.
They often interrupt and respond before a person is finished. When things
don't go fast enough to their liking, they become angry. They consider
themselves hard-working and responsible: they struggle with laziness.
They hate not being trusted and do not always keep their commitments and
promises or forces themselves to keep them. They tend to be impatient and
intolerant. They confide with difficulty and do not show their vulnerability.

People with a betrayal wound have great difficulty accepting the cowardice
of others. They also have trouble delegating tasks while trusting others.
Among the five wounds, the betrayal wounded is the one who has the most
expectations towards others because he likes to foresee and control
everything. Unlike abandonment wounded who has expectations of others
because they want to be loved and supported in their abandonment injury,
the expectations of the betrayal wounded are to check that others do what
they need to do well to verify if they can trust them.

They firmly state what they believe and expect others to agree with their
beliefs. They tend to state their point of view categorically and seeks to

convince others at all costs. They think that when someone understands them, they agree with them, which unfortunately is not always the case. Their biggest fears are disengagement, separation, dissociation, and denial, which are often experienced in a situation of betrayal.

It is essential to know what your wounds are to identify your limits and

what
obstacles stop you from being your true self. By being aware of your behaviors and wounds, you are getting to know yourself better and also understanding why you tend to behave in specific ways. Maybe one of your wounds is betrayal, and you get very insecure in your relationship when your partner doesn't live up to your expectations, by knowing that about yourself, you can learn to improve the relationship and how you react to certain situations.

The first step to heal your wounds is to observe yourself when you feel hurt (chapter 10 will help you with that). Then you can move on to accept that you aren't perfect, and it's OK to recognize the hurt. Last is to admit your fear and allow yourself to move through that fear by being vulnerable and honest with yourself and others.

"Whether you think you can or think you can't. You're right."
Henry Ford

CHAPTER 5
CREATE BOUNDARIES

CHAPTER 5: CREATE BOUNDARIES

Boundaries are one of the most underused ways to be the best version of yourself. You must learn to say "no." Saying "no' is probably one of the hardest things you'll ever have to do to ensure you are in integrity with yourself.

Most people are not used to hearing "no" or even respect the word "no." To learn to say "no," you have to explore how you react to people who say "no" to you. Once you are open to others saying "no" to you, start practicing it yourself. Say "no" when you don't feel like doing something or when it doesn't feel right for you.

Another aspect of creating boundaries is how you behave in your friendship circle. Be clear about individuals who are supportive and uplift you and stay away from those who only bring you down, or feed drama. Surround yourself with people who appreciate you for who you truly are. Now is the perfect time to assess your friendships and set boundaries around those who do not complete you.

Toxic relationships often feel a more deep-seated need to please others. If you are experiencing a relationship with a person who is mean to you or always makes you feel bad about yourself, know that you are allowing this. It is OK for you to say "no" to that type of relationship. It doesn't have to be a romantic relationship; it could be with a friend or a coworker.

To have healthy boundaries, you need to know what you value. If you value compassion, but you turn around and start criticizing and gossiping with a friend, you are not in integrity with yourself. Be clear about what you value and then match the behaviors to those values. That way, it will be easier to create boundaries and shift your behavior when it is not aligned with your values and beliefs. Once you are clear with your values, seek them in others, and surround yourself with people who have similar values to you.

Once you can recognize how you feel about the relationship you currently have and are clear about your values, it will be much easier to assert yourself. For example, if you are with a group of friends and one suggests something you are uncomfortable about, you can assert yourself.

Express how you feel and why you don't feel like participating in that idea. The more you will assert yourself, the better you will feel about yourself. Just be mindful that you are not judging or criticizing others when you assert yourself. Position your thoughts in a way that it's about what you feel and what you don't feel is aligned with your true self.

But most of all, stop trying to please others because it is one of the most limiting behaviors you can have. When you please others, you completely forget your true self and allow others to dictate how you should behave, look, and even talk. This type of behavior is very destructive to the self, and it is pretty much "acting" yourself. You become an actor and live the life that others want you to live in.

Once you learn to let go of pleasing others, you start living your own life. You no longer tailor your experience to the image of others but more to what you want and who you are. By doing so, the people around you will accept you for who you are, and if they don't accept you, they are not meant to be in your life.

Creating boundaries means recognizing that sometimes you do things to please others, and that has to stop if it makes you feel bad about yourself. Pay attention to when you say "yes," and deep down, you don't feel like doing something. Take the courage to stop trying to please others. For example, if somebody asks you to do something for them and you don't feel it's aligned with your needs, just say that it's not a good time for you. You can also say "no."

Doing what you want doesn't mean free for all; it means showing compassion toward what lies in your heart and do things that bring you joy, fulfillment, and drive. The more you will do things that bring you joy, the less you will need boundaries; you will surround yourself with people who appreciate you for who you are. You won't need to say "no" because it will be aligned with your true self.

Once you start setting boundaries, you will notice your life-changing, and you will find yourself experiencing more positive moments. A life with boundaries is the perfect environment to be yourself and live your best life.

If you want to be the best version of yourself, you need to learn to say no and create boundaries. By distancing yourself from things that don't align with your authentic self, you are saying no to distraction and hindrance to living your best life.

When you start respecting yourself, you put yourself as the priority. Many people believe it is selfish; meanwhile, when it is done for the right reasons, it serves a bigger purpose. It allows you to have the time, energy, and wellness to be your best self around others.

It will enable you to be present for others and, in return, uplift them too. When you find the courage to create healthy boundaries in your life, you quickly are rewarded with joy, happiness, and a sense of becoming the best version of yourself.

"Setting boundaries is a way of caring for myself. It doesn't make me mean, selfish, or uncaring (just) because I don't do things your way. I care about me too.
Christine Morgan

CHAPTER 6
INCREASE YOUR SELF-CONFIDENCE AND SELF-ESTEEM

CHAPTER 6: INCREASE YOUR SELF-CONFIDENCE AND SELF-ESTEEM

Self-confidence is mostly behavior-based, and it is about knowing what your abilities are while self-esteem is more mind based on how you perceive yourself. Self-esteem and self-confidence are not always positively correlated. For example, you can be good at something and trust your skills (self-confidence) but still perceive yourself as a loser (self-esteem). First, let's explore self-confidence and assess how your self-confidence is.

Self-Confidence

Self-confidence is about trusting your abilities and also trust your own judgment and decisions. People with low self-confidence will judge themselves by their actions or what they are incapable of doing. When you experience low self-confidence, you will likely see the gaps in yourself.

Here are some questions that will help you assess your self-confidence (check all that applies to you).

   I do what is expected of me even when it doesn't necessarily feel right.
   I often feel sad and discourage about my life.
   It's hard for me to handle change.
   When something looks hard, I usually don't even try it.
   I rarely set goals for myself.
   I rarely find solutions to my problems.

When I receive feedback, I often feel hopeless.
Obstacles are failures for me.
I can't list five of my qualities right now.
I feel like I don't have the abilities, resources, and skills to accomplish your goals.
I rarely take a risk because that often means failure for me.

The more answers you've checked, the more you need to work on your self-confidence.

One of the easiest ways to work on self-confidence is to assess your level of comfort at accepting compliments from others and correct it. How do you react when someone gives you a compliment or positive feedback? Most people who struggle with that will show a lower level of self-confidence.

Correcting this is simple: learn to respond with "Thank You." Stop making excuses or reasons for it, and simply say thank you. This will improve your relationship with others and, mostly, with yourself. If you can't accept compliments from others, how can you expect to recognize your qualities? Start by showing a different behavior in your external world and the inner world will positively change.

Another way to build self-confidence is to strengthen your self-esteem, which is more the way you perceive yourself. Improve your perception of yourself, and you are less likely to see the gaps in your behaviors.

Self-Esteem

Self-esteem is the way we perceive or evaluate our worth and is the ultimate belief we place on ourselves. People with high self-esteem tend to be more comfortable with their true selves and demonstrate a lot more integrity.

When we have high self-esteem, we respect our true selves. On the other hand, people with low self-esteem will often stop themselves from doing something or from expressing who they are because they fear that they will not be accepted and love for who they are.

Our fear of being judged often lead us to behave in a way that is not aligned with what our heart wants because we want to feel accepted and loved by others. To get over this fear, you have to let go of the need for approval from others slowly. You can do so by taking the time to accept yourself first, and then you can express who you are without feeling like others will judge you.

Let's evaluate your level of self-esteem; check all that applies to you.

I am comfortable and happy to be myself
I recognize my qualities and skills
I have a lot of respect for who I am
I can be as valuable as any other person
I enjoy being myself, as opposed to a persona to please others
Failure is not something I see in myself; Instead, I see failures as opportunities for growth
I feel that I am worthwhile
I can look at myself in the mirror and feel comfortable and loving toward myself
I don't expect everyone to like me and that is OK, I don't feel the need to change for them
I'm always open for growth and yet, love and accept myself as I am
I can be my biggest fan

The more answers you've checked, the higher is your self-esteem. To develop your self-esteem, you can work on the following.

Appreciate Yourself

Appreciating yourself means that you are OK with who you are and enjoy being by yourself. Have the goal of becoming your best friend. Take some time to hang out with yourself once in a while. It will help you build a level of comfort in being by yourself. Add some self-care during those moments; it will help you increase self-respect.

Be Proud of Your Accomplishments

We've all accomplished something in our life. It could be as simple as completing your elementary school or getting that job you applied for. Whatever it is, take the time to list the things you've accomplished in your life, even if it is as simple as making your bed!

Recognize Your Skills

Every one of us is good at something. If it's hard for you to identify those skills, ask someone around you to help list a few abilities that you have. It can be hard skills like carpentry, drawing, or cooking. It could also be a soft skill like listening, compassion, or empathy.

Learn to Love Your Body

Learning to love our bodies is probably one of the most significant accomplishments we can make in our life. Some studies show that 40% of men and over 90% of women are unhappy with their bodies. That is almost unreal! Loving your body is about self-talk (which will be covered in chapter 9) but also about self-respect. Be your best friend and treat your body the same way you would treat your child or best friend. Be kind, compassionate, and supportive.

Compassion toward ourselves will often lead to better self-esteem and higher self-confidence. There is also an aspect of connecting with the self that becomes important. This is the subject of the next chapter.

"One can only hope the person you love will make you the best version of yourself."
Mia Maestro

CHAPTER 7
CONNECTING WITH YOUR AUTHENTICITY

CHAPTER 7: CONNECTING WITH YOUR AUTHENTICITY

Authentic people are genuine, real, and mostly, in integrity with themselves. They don't try to be someone they are not or please people they don't know. They, in some ways, know that they are unique but accept that aspect of themselves. For them, being different is not an issue nor something they thrive to be; they are just themselves.

Authentic people also love doing what they enjoy and don't try to copy others' ideas for the sake of being successful. Their success comes from doing what is in their heart, what drives them, as opposed to what inspire others or the majority.

One of the best ways to connect with your authentic self is to stop comparing yourself to others. When you compare yourself to others, you automatically feed a belief that you should be like others, that being yourself is not enough. This limits you from being yourself and making it OK. Most of us often compare ourselves to others because we have that belief that others have it better than us. This can transform into envy or jealousy.

Take a moment to list all the things that make you happy and fulfill a space in your heart:

____

____

____

____

____

____

____

____

Now find ways to do more of that. When you do the things that you love, you are being authentic, you are exposing the best version of yourself, andthat's why it is fulfilling. Another way to reconnect with your true and authentic self is to rediscover your inner child, the one that didn't care about what others thought.

"Authenticity is the daily practice of letting go of who we think we're supposed to be and embracing who we are."
Brené Brown

CHAPTER 8
RECONNECTING WITH
YOUR INNER CHILD

CHAPTER 8: RECONNECTING WITH YOUR INNER CHILD

When you reconnect with your inner child, you also heal wounds from the past (often associated with the five wounds in chapter 4.). The top things you can learn from your inner child are the following:

There is no such thing as failures, only experiences. The best way to experience life is through play.

It doesn't matter what others think. If you want to scream, scream; if you want to dance in public, dance in public; if you want to sing when you eat, sing when you eat.

Love is unconditional. I love my parents no matter what or who they are, from the moment I am born.

I live in the present moment. When I am hungry, you know it; When I am happy, you know it; When I am calm, you know it. I am not afraid to express how I feel.

It's easy to forgive others; you just have to show compassion and move on.

Try to be more like your inner child and awaken that aspect of you that you knew when you were young, but somehow, you've disconnected from growing up. Take the time to play again, to make mistakes, forgive and try something else. Don't be afraid to be vulnerable and do what your heart tells you to do, no matter what others may think. Love yourself and others around you learn to love unconditionally once again, show compassion to those around you. And most of all, learn to live in the present moment, stop resisting all those emotions and learn to express them more healthily (and not repress).

"The most potent muse of all is our own inner child."
Stephen Nachmanovitch

BECOMING THE BEST VERSION OF YOURSELF
CHAPTER 9
TAME YOUR INNER VOICE

CHAPTER 9: TAME YOUR INNER VOICE

Self-talk is one of the most powerful forms of communication because it has the power to lift you up or bring you down in a matter of seconds.

It is often impressive how we can be mean to ourselves. While most of us would never express hate or diminishing words toward our friends and families, yet, we let ourselves be our biggest bully.

The first step is to pay attention to your inner chat. What are the thoughts that cross your mind when you look at yourself in the mirror or when you make a mistake? Be aware that if you practice negative self-talk, this didn't happen overnight, and it will require a lot of practice, awareness, and work to get the habit out of you.

Second, try to identify when you are using a lot of negative self-talk.

Is it when you look at yourself in the mirror?

When you are out with friends or when you are at work?

Once you've identified it, make a new affirmation that will replace your negative self-talk.

For example, if you are always criticizing yourself when you are at the gym (ex: that your hips are too big or your belly is not in enough), make a new phrase in your mind that you will use when you are exercising. It could be that you are proud of yourself for taking the time to take care of your physical body. Be aware of your negative chatter and change it to something more positive.

> "Self-talk reflects your innermost feelings." Asa Don Brown

CHAPTER 10
INCREASE YOUR
SELF-AWARENESS

CHAPTER 10: INCREASE YOUR SELF-AWARENESS

Have you ever been in a public space, and the person next to you express this huge sigh that clearly shows her impatience toward the situation? How did that make you feel? Were you a bit uncomfortable?

That person didn't care about self-awareness. Self-awareness is the ability to recognize your emotional state and find ways to stay in balance. When you practice self-awareness, you are automatically allowing yourself to be a better version of yourself and not let your emotions take control of you.

Being self-aware simply means that you can observe yourself from a non-judgmental perspective.

When you are self-aware, you can catch yourself in the present moment experiencing a specific state, reaction, or feeling.

The more you are aware of your emotions, the more you start to understand yourself.

For example, you might observe that you tend to be reactive when someone provides you with a suggestion on how to do something different. When you are aware of your emotions, you have a better idea of who you are and how you tend to react in certain situations. It is also the best way to improve yourself on certain aspects that you don't find optimal. You become less driven by drama.

Self-awareness will help you in your daily life with identifying moments when you are living one of the five wounds, or when you are a victim and not aligned with the best version of yourself. Self-awareness will also help you with the following:

Experience a greater ability to recognize your emotions

Improve your critical thinking

Improve your relationships

Live in the present moment

Experience more joy and happiness

But the ultimate reward to being self-aware is your ability to recognize when you are not in alignment with your true self. It is the opportunity to be authentic and therefore be in integrity with yourselves. Self-awareness is the key to becoming the best version of yourself.

"Awareness is the greatest agent for change."
Eckart Tolle

5 Steps
You Can Take Today
For
Becoming The Best
Version of
Yourself

Want to become the best version of you? Or at least to begin taking the necessary steps to start being more productive, more creative, happier and more confident?

There are plenty of ways to do that and some of them involve taking a deep look at yourself and discovering who you really are and what you really want from life.

But while this can work, there are also some much more practical and straightforward strategies you can use to keep growing and improving yourself. In this short report, we'll be looking at the five things you should do if you want to keep yourself growing and improving. These are concrete steps that anyone can take but which can't help to improve and develop you over time.

1.) Learn

One of the most important things you can do to keep developing and growing yourself is to learn. That means that you should keep on taking on new challenges, discovering new things and developing new skills and abilities.

Maybe you attend an electronic engineering seminar. Maybe you go to dance classes. Maybe you teach yourself to use a new piece of software to further your career. Or maybe you learn a new language.

Whichever of these options you choose, continuing to learn will help to make your brain more plastic as it produces neurotransmitters associated with the growth and development of neurons and neuronal connections. You'll produce more brain derived neurotrophic factor, more dopamine, more norepinephrine and more. And as a result, you will find *all* new topics easier to learn and your brain will be more similar to that of a much younger person's.

The same is true for the brain as is for the body: you can either grow and improve, or you can atrophy and deteriorate. The body is always changing: it is simply up to you whether it changes for the better or for the worse.

And if nothing else, continually learning new things will give you a broader mind, a wider range of experiences and skills to draw upon and a ton of useful knowledge. And the new ideas and concepts that you can come up with as a result of combining experience from many different fields is almost limitless. This is how you become a 'polymath' like Da Vinci, Newton or Elon Musk.

Make Time to Learn!

2.) Travel

Travelling is incredibly important not only for your happiness and your sense of accomplishment and purpose, but also to make you a more rounded and even a more decent human being.

Did you know that people are rated as more tolerant and understanding if they went to college? This has nothing to do with education or background – it is simply that people who have moved away from home have less narrow views and a better understanding of the wider world.

And this is even truer for those people who travel far and wide and mingle with other cultures and see other places for themselves. This broadens your mind and gives you a 'bigger picture' view. It can also help you to put things in perspective a little and to realize that many of your troubles and your concerns are actually somewhat petty in comparison to the hunger and poverty you encounter in other parts of the world.

People who have travelled and had adventures will be naturally more interesting to talk to because they'll have such a breadth of experiences to share and because they'll appear more worldly and more knowledgeable. But it's simply rubbing shoulders with people from different cultures and experiencing unique locales that will truly develop you.

To get a little deeper in our understanding of how travelling can change and improve a person, it pays to consider the philosophies of Georg Hegel. Hegel believed that it was crucial that we challenge our ideas in order to develop them and to gain a more accurate world view. He described this as requiring a specific process. The 'thesis' is the original idea that you have. The antithesis is the opposite view. And the synthesis is the resultant idea that takes lessons from both views.

In order for us to be as knowledgeable and as effective as possible, it is crucial that we challenge our existing ideas and develop them by incorporating other ideas.
Refusal to do this otherwise will eventually result in our own demise, as we become more and more attached to defunct and irrelevant concepts.

Without these outside views and experiences to challenge us, we simply become more and more extreme in our own views. This happens through 'confirmation bias' as we seek out more knowledge to confirm what we already hold to be true. And it happens through 'convergence' and 'divergence', the likelihood of in-groups becoming more similar to each other and less similar to outgroups.

We can look to nature for a great analogy. In nature, the single most important thing for the survival of our DNA is diversity. We seek mates for procreation because they are different from us and because they introduce new genetic material into our makeup. If we continually in-bread, then the flaws and imperfections in our DNA become exaggerated to the point that we can even become deformed or unwell as a species!

Conversely, having offspring with people of different cultures and from different regions will create stronger DNA that is less prone to illness.

The same goes for our ideas. This is why it is so good for us as a species to overcome borders and differences and to interact with others that are diverse and varied as possible. By challenging and constantly reassessing your ideas and beliefs, you will come out with stronger, more accurate and more useful ideas and beliefs.

Travel is one of the greatest things you can do for the mind and the soul.

3.) Meditate

If there's one new habit you should consider adopting, then it is meditation. Meditation is simply practiced focus and concentration. Here, you will put yourself in a quiet environment and then focus on clearing your mind of distracting and unwanted thoughts. You will be ruminating on stressful topics, and you will gradually become better at focusing and remaining calm.

This is an incredibly powerful skill because it gives you the ability to rise above stress and panic and to remain calm no matter what is going on around you. This can make you a happier individual, as you'll be less bothered by hard days at work or large deadlines but it can also make you more effective as you gain greater control over your emotional response, more emotional stability and the ability to concentrate more effectively on given tasks.

And did you know that meditation physically changes the structure of the brain? It has been demonstrated to increase 'cortical thickness', which means that there is more grey matter and a greater density of neural connections. Studies also show that meditation can improve concentration, focus, emotional stability and even IQ. In other words, meditating makes you a more focused and even more intelligent individual.

This can be a difficult habit to get into, especially if you are someone who is unfamiliar with how meditation works, or perhaps who has never considered it in the past.

The simplest form of mediation is mindfulness meditation. Here, you simply sit somewhere quietly and 'watch' your thoughts go by. The idea is to allow them to pass by like clouds without engaging in them or worrying about their content. Don't punish yourself for letting your mind wander, just make a note of the thought and then dismiss it. Not only does this teach you to rise above your thoughts and be less concerned by them but it also helps you to gain a greater understanding of the contents of your own mind so that you can predict your own reactions to future scenarios.

If you struggle to find the time necessary to commit, then try meditating for just 7 minutes a day. This amount of time is short enough that you should be able to slip it in without too much difficulty but it will be enough to start causing significant changes to the way your brain works.

4.) Exercise

It might not be the most exciting or even surprising item on this list, but it is nevertheless absolutely crucial that exercise be part of your routine. Exercise is not just important as a way to get more physically fit: it can actually change your hormonal balance and even your brain in profoundly positive ways. Did you know that exercise – both CV and resistance training – can actually boost your IQ and increase your concentration? One possible explanation for how resistance training might accomplish this is by helping with 'embodied cognition'. Embodied cognition is a theory as to the working of the brain that suggests we actually understand things by using our bodies and our memories of our interactions with the world: when we hear a story about someone being cold, we actually remember what it is like to be cold and even feel it slightly with our bodies.

Training can strengthen your connection with your body and in doing this, it will make you better at using it to understand foreign concepts.

At the same time, getting into better shape will improve your energy levels, will help you to sleep better, will make you less prone to illness, will make you more attractive, will enable you to look better in your clothes, will raise your confidence, will improve your physical performance in sports and competition, will make you better able to take care of yourself in a physical confrontation and much, much more.

Again, you don't need to commit to huge amounts of exercise right away. Just a few workouts a week can be enough to start making a difference and you can take this relatively gently at least to begin with!

5.) Grooming and Style

Everything else on this list has been about making yourself healthier, calmer and more worldly. These are deep changes that will affect you from the inside out. But grooming and taking care of your sense of style is different. This is an example of a change that happens from the outside in: it's something immediate and easy you can change about yourself that will then begin to make you feel better on the inside.

What I'm trying to say is: don't write this off as something trite and shallow. Looking after your appearance is essentially a way to invest in yourself and to demonstrate that you place value in your appearance. This sends a powerful signal to others that makes you seem more capable, more confident and much more attractive. As a result, it can help you to increase your chances of getting a job interview, of attracting a member of the opposite sex and of walking into a room and turning heads for all the right reasons.

What's more, is that the sense of confidence you gain from looking and feeling great can help you to feel better about yourself and to be happier and more content as a result.

Start by choosing to invest a little more financially into what you wear and how you groom yourself. It's better to have fewer clothes but for those clothes to be better made. And they say that your haircut should directly reflect the amount of money that you're responsible for in your career. Ever heard the expression 'dress for the job you want'?

Consider speaking with a style advisor, certainly be willing to get slightly out of your comfort zone and find a time to groom yourself regularly. Oh and definitely invest in the future: if you want to feel amazing in 10 years time, then moisturizing and protecting yourself from the sun will make a big help!

CONCLUSION

CONCLUSION

Being the best version of yourself is not an objective that we can reach overnight. As a human being, we first have to accept that we aren't perfect, and perfection will never be our truth. As you have learned from this book, becoming the best version of yourself is not about perfection but more about finding your true self.

The true self can only be found when we choose to remove the mask that we've been wearing for a long time. That mask comes with behaviors and wounds that only time and hard work can heal. Don't be afraid to face your shadows and bring to light the aspect of yourself that needs to heal.

Never forget that human's were never meant to be alone and do things on their own. We are social creatures that require a community to thrive. Don't hesitate to seek help from experts or build a support network for encouraging and motivating you to grow.

Every month, try to redo the assessment that is located in chapter 1, it will be a great way to identify if you are getting closer to being the best version of yourself. That assessment will also help you determine which area still needs more work and why not make a goal out of it! No matter what, you got this and embrace the best version of yourself today!

With all these changes you will slowly begin to evolve from the inside and outside. You will look and act more confident and capable and you will feel healthier, more full of energy and stronger all at the same time. Just 5 steps and you can begin your self-transformation!